Science Detectives

How scientists solved six real-life mysteries

By the Editors of *YES Mag*

Illustrated by Rose Cowles

Kids Can Press

To Tobin, my secret weapon. — J.I.
To Ally and Brad, thanks for the encouraging
words! — M.K.

Acknowledgments
Special thanks to: Judith W. Leavitt, Rupple-Bascom and Ruth
Bleier Professor of Medical History and Women's Studies,
University of Wisconsin; Dr. Lindsay Oaks, DVM, Ph.D.,
College of Veterinary Medicine, Washington State University;
Rick Watson, International Programs Director, The Peregrine
Fund; Stephen T. Johnston, School of Earth and Ocean
Sciences, University of Victoria; Dr. Eduard Egarter Vigl,
South Tyrol Museum of Archaeology, Bolzano, Italy; Dr. Ben F.
Koop, Professor and Director, Centre for Biomedical Research,
University of Victoria.

The YES Mag team members who worked on this book are
Jude Isabella and Megan Kopp.

Kids Can Press acknowledges the financial support of the
Government of Ontario, through the Ontario Media Development
Corporation's Ontario Book Initiative; the Ontario Arts Council;
the Canada Council for the Arts; and the Government of Canada,
through the CBF, for our publishing activity.

Published in Canada by
Kids Can Press Ltd.
25 Dockside Drive
Toronto, ON M5A 0B5

Published in the U.S. by
Kids Can Press Ltd.
2250 Military Road
Tonawanda, NY 14150

www.kidscanpress.com

Edited by Valerie Wyatt
Designed by Julia Naimska
Illustrations by Rose Cowles

The hardcover edition of this book is smyth sewn casebound.
The paperback edition of this book is limp sewn with a
drawn-on cover.
Manufactured in Buji, Shenzhen, China, in 8/2012 by WKT
Company

CM 06 0 9 8 7 6 5 4 3
CM PA 06 0 9 8 7 6 5

Library and Archives Canada Cataloguing in Publication

Science detectives / by the editors of Yes mag ; illustrated
by Rose Cowles.

Includes index.
ISBN 978-1-55337-994-2 (bound)
ISBN 978-1-55337-995-9 (pbk.)

1. Science—Methodology—Juvenile literature. I. Cowles,
Rose, 1967–

Q163.S363 2006   j501   C2006-900166-9

Kids Can Press is a *Corus*™ Entertainment company

Photo Credits
Every reasonable effort has been made to trace ownership of
and give accurate credit to copyrighted material. Information
that would enable the publisher to correct any discrepancies
in future editions would be appreciated.

Abbreviations
t = top; b = bottom; l = left; r = right

p. 5: (butterfly) Corax Networks Inc.; p. 7: Science
Source/Photo Researchers, Inc.; p. 9: (t) Val Wyatt; p. 15: (t)
The Peregrine Fund; p. 16: (l, r) The Peregrine Fund; p. 19:
Peter Scoones/Photo/Researchers, Inc.; p. 21: Photo Archives,
South Tyrol Museum of Archaeology; p. 23: Photo Archives,
South Tyrol Museum of Archaeology; p. 25: (l, r) Chris
Turney/University of Wollongong; p. 27: J. Steeves/Parks
Canada; p. 28: Courtesy Metalex Labs; p. 31: (b) Earth
Sciences Information Centre/Natural Resources Canada;
p. 33: Marli Miller; p. 37: A. Barrington Brown/Photo
Researchers, Inc.; p. 38: Omikron/Photo Researchers, Inc.;
p. 40: Photo Researchers, Inc.; p. 42: J. Wyte/Ivy Images;
p. 43: (t) Transportation Safety Board of Canada; p. 43:
(b) G. Daigle/Ivy Images; p. 45: Transportation Safety Board
of Canada; p. 46: (t, b) NASA. All other photos © 2006
Jupiterimages Corporation.

Contents

The Case of the Sleuthing Scientists

The world is a place of mystery. To unravel its secrets, scientists must think like detectives.

When confronted with a puzzle — Why are your eyes brown? Why did that plane crash? Why is everyone getting sick? — scientists look for clues. Clues lead to facts. When you have lots of facts, you have evidence. And scientists use evidence to reveal the truth behind a mystery.

Turn the page and find out how some of the most mind-boggling riddles were solved by scientific detectives …

The Case of the Contaminated Cook

Long Island, New York, 1906. Ah, summer! Sun, surf … and typhoid. At least that's how it was for Charles Warren, a New York City banker who was banking on a good time when he rented a summer place for his family.

By the end of August, typhoid fever had struck six out of eleven people in the Warren household. The youngest daughter, Margaret, was the first to crawl into bed with a high fever, splitting headache and diarrhea. Eventually her mother, sister, two maids and the gardener slid into the same feverish delirium. They were not enjoying their summer vacation in the large, beautiful home owned by George Thompson.

Thompson's summer began to look bleak, too. Typhoid is contagious, and Thompson knew that no one would rent the house once the Warrens left. And worse, typhoid houses were sometimes burned to the ground in an effort to get rid of the disease.

Terrible Typhoid

Salmonella typhi is a bacterium that causes typhoid fever. The disease was a common menace in North America in the early 1900s. It was often spread through contaminated food or water. The bustling city of Chicago was dubbed Typhoid Fever City. Two epidemics swept through Toronto while the city fiddled with the public water system. (Residents called the reservoir water "drinkable sewage.") In New York City, roughly four thousand new cases of typhoid were reported every year.

But poor people in crowded spaces with inadequate sanitation were the usual typhoid victims, not the rich. Long Island and typhoid? Presidents summered there for goodness' sake!

George Thompson called in some medical experts. They were quick on the draw. Typhoid? Surely it was the drinking water. But a search for typhoid germs turned up nothing. The one indoor toilet, the outhouse and the animal manure pile were all analyzed. Again, nothing. Milk and cheese were suspected next. No luck. Clams! The family loved clams and often bought them from locals. Maybe the shellfish came from a polluted bay. Yet the neighbors also munched on the same clams, and they didn't get sick.

Thompson needed the medical equivalent of Sherlock Holmes, fast.

THE TYPHOID SOURCES???
- Doo-doo in the drinking water?
- A leaky outhouse or toilet?
- Manure-laced munchies?
- Contaminated clams?

Case # 4739

Tracing Typhoid

Typhoid probably originated in rodents and birds. It's one of many diseases caused by salmonella — a group of bacteria that live in warm-blooded species.

Eat something contaminated with *Salmonella typhi* and a week later you're running a high fever, clutching your head and belly in pain and running to the toilet. You might also be coughing. Children make up the majority of typhoid victims.

Today, about four hundred cases are reported yearly in the United States, but these typhoid victims are usually infected while traveling elsewhere.

Typhoid is found mostly in poor countries. Worldwide, there are up to twenty-two million new cases per year, with two hundred thousand deaths. Typhoid is easily controlled by cleaning up sewer systems and water supplies, but making these improvements costs money that many developing nations do not have.

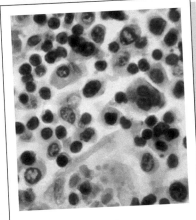

Typhoid bacteria

The Carrier Culprit

Enter Dr. George Soper. At age thirty-six, Dr. Soper was a no-nonsense New York City sanitation engineer and expert epidemiologist (a person who tracks the spread of diseases). He had solved other mysterious epidemics in 1903 and 1904. And he was known to burn down a house or two to eradicate typhoid.

The Warren case intrigued Soper — only ten previous cases of typhoid had ever been reported in the Oyster Bay area prior to the Warrens' unfortunate summer vacation. Soper interviewed the Warrens and their servants. He even pored over a list of house visitors going back ten years. Researching the medical histories of the visitors, Soper found that no seriously sick person had even visited the house in those years, and there was certainly no history of typhoid. Strange. Typhoid sources usually turn up easily when you know where to look.

Soper concentrated again on the current household's activities. Perhaps Margaret Warren and the others had gotten sick after a visit somewhere else. It was another dead end. No one had gone anywhere for weeks.

Margaret, however, took sick August 27. Soper reasoned that around August 20, the bacterium must have been lurking in the food she ate. But how did it get there?

Soper checked with the kitchen staff. The family had changed cooks on August 4. Cooks handle food. Could the cook be the missing piece of the puzzle?

According to the family, the new cook, Mary Mallon, had showed no typhoid symptoms. Still, from reading medical journals, Soper knew that a healthy person could spread typhoid. These people are called "carriers" — they never notice they have the disease, or they have a full-blown case and recover but still carry the bacteria.

Soper focused on Mallon, who had since moved on. He asked more detailed questions of the staff and family. For three weeks Mallon had made breakfast, lunch and dinner in the posh home's kitchen. Typhoid germs are usually killed when heated. But before Margaret and the others had fallen ill, Mallon had put together a dessert of fresh peaches and ice cream. No cooking involved. Then the cook was gone, leaving behind illness, but no forwarding address.

Case # 1623

Disease Trackers

Epidemiologists track diseases. They study the spread of diseases and try to stop them cold — before they cause an epidemic.

The World Health Organization has teams of epidemiologists who "spy" on diseases, everything from obesity epidemics to infectious illnesses like polio. Disease-hunters fan out across the globe, tracking diseases and, if possible, getting rid of them through vaccination programs. You can't vaccinate against obesity, but measles, whooping cough and polio can all be tamed.

Vaccines ended the life of smallpox in 1979. They also limit epidemics of cholera, typhoid and the ever-changing influenza (flu) virus.

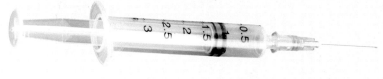

To Catch a Cook

Mary Mallon was described as Irish, in her late thirties, intelligent, single and in perfect health. Soper knew Mallon was his most important lead — he needed to find and question her.

Soper approached the employment agency that helped Mallon find work. He studied her employment history and questioned past employers, servants, friends — anyone who knew Mallon. In the ten years she had been a cook, Mallon worked for eight families, seven of which had developed cases of typhoid.

Mallon was looking awfully suspicious. Soper wanted to talk to her, but she had disappeared.

Soper scoured the city and found the cook at a ritzy Park Avenue residence. On February 23, 1907, the daughter of the house died of typhoid fever. Mary Mallon had started cooking for the family two months earlier. Time to pay the cook a visit, reasoned Soper. Surely Mallon would want to know if she was giving people typhoid.

It was a short interview. Soper, not known for his tact, demanded stool and urine samples to test for typhoid. Mallon thought he was a nut case. The blond, blue-eyed cook — the picture of health — grabbed a carving fork and chased him. Soper ran.

For the next meeting, Soper took along a doctor friend. They stopped Mallon on the way to a friend's house. She was a carrier, the doctor duo explained, but Mallon blew her stack, and the two men gave up. It seemed hopeless. Time to bring in the big guns.

Dr. S. Josephine Baker, a medical inspector with the New York Department of Health, visited Mallon, asking for specimens. Mallon slammed the door in her face. The next day, Baker was back, with several police officers. Mallon escaped. After hours of searching, the cook was found hiding in a neighbor's closet. The police dragged her to an ambulance. With Baker literally sitting on Mallon, and Mallon cursing and ranting, the cook was brought to the hospital. Finally she relented and gave urine, blood and stool samples. Her stools were teeming with the bacteria. She was, as Soper had guessed, a typhoid carrier. And it didn't help that Mallon was less than thorough when she washed her hands after using the toilet.

Shoo, Flu

In May 1997, a three-year-old boy in Hong Kong went to the hospital with a cough and high fever. He was struggling to breathe. The laboratory confirmed the worst: a new type of influenza virus, called avian flu.

Influenza, usually called flu, causes fever, fatigue and muscle aches. In the very young and very old, it often allows deadly pneumonia bacteria into the lungs. The flu virus is constantly changing, so a new vaccination is needed each year. But every eight to forty years the virus does something unique — it totally rearranges its genetic make-up and becomes a brand new type of flu. With no available vaccine and no immunity, the new strain can cause a pandemic (a global epidemic) in which people worldwide get sick. The 1918 influenza pandemic killed between twenty million and forty million people. And modern travel means viruses can hitch a ride via jet, landing anywhere in the world within hours.

Wild ducks are the main flu carriers. Avian (bird) flu can be fast and fatal for domestic birds, such as chickens, while humans are unaffected. This avian virus, however, had jumped directly from a bird to the boy, probably through pet chicks kept at his preschool. The chicks fell ill and died. So did the boy. He was one of six deaths out of the eighteen people who came down with avian flu in Hong Kong that year. Epidemiologists were shocked; they had to track down the virus's origin.

Flu-hunters went into overdrive. A study revealed that 10 percent of the chickens in the food market had the virus, as did wild geese and ducks. Ah ha! Slaughter the chickens and a major source of the bird flu virus would disappear.

Within three days, over a million chickens were gassed or had their throats slit. The flu strain was stopped or at least slowed down, but it was just the beginning of a new flu era. Avian flu came back to stay two years later, and epidemiologists are still trying to track down — and stop — new outbreaks.

Chickens can be infected with avian flu by migrating ducks and geese.

Confining the Cook

When news hit the papers, Mary Mallon was soon nicknamed Typhoid Mary. Back in 1907 there were no antibiotics to treat her, and almost every sample she ever gave turned up typhoid. She was the first healthy carrier ever identified, although hundreds were eventually discovered. For three years Typhoid Mary was a prisoner, held at a hospital. She was the only healthy carrier ever confined.

Public pressure forced the release of Mallon, and she promised never to cook again. She washed clothes instead. It was a low-paying job, much less glamorous than being a cook. She changed her name and disappeared.

But then, in 1915, a prestigious maternity hospital needed Soper's services. Twenty-five cases of typhoid fever had erupted, mostly among doctors and nurses. A few interviews later Soper knew who the culprit was. It was the hospital's cook — Typhoid Mary "Brown."

Tracked down again, the cook offered no resistance. She was confined to a one-room cottage on hospital grounds for good. In 1932, she had a stroke. Typhoid Mary died five years later, after twenty-three years of confinement. She had infected at least fifty-one people and caused three deaths.

Pass the Soap

The American Society of Microbiology reports that only 39 percent of Americans wash their hands after sneezing or coughing. So if you shook hands with four people during the cold season, two of them might have contaminated hands. Yuck.

Touch your eyes, nose or mouth after touching a contaminated person or thing and you're giving germs a pathway into your body. Infectious diseases — colds, flu and intestinal illnesses — are often spread hand-to-hand. To stop the spread of germs, wash your hands frequently. Here's how to do it: Use lots of soap and warm water. Lather up to your wrists. Rub your hands together thoroughly while singing "Happy Birthday" twice. Rinse. Dry. Smile — you're germ-free.

Project 1: All Washed Up

Ask people if they wash their hands after using the toilet and almost all of them will say yes. So researchers stationed themselves at major airports in the United States and watched.

They found that more than 10 percent of the people did *not* wash their hands after using the toilet.

Station yourself in your school washroom for fifteen minutes — try to look inconspicuous — and record how many people leave without washing their hands. Are your numbers the same — do one out of ten people not wash their hands?

The Case of the Vanishing Vultures

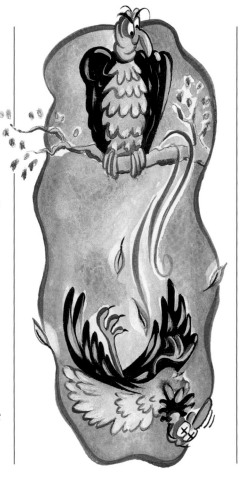

About seventy of them hiss and grunt, tugging and pulling at dead flesh. They dance around with outstretched wings, jostling each other to get the best bit — and in minutes the vultures strip the cow carcass to mere bones.

Not a pretty sight, but these peacock-sized birds are a great clean-up crew. That's important when you live in a country with a lot of cows raised for their milk, not their meat. Think India, where dead cattle are left in the field for vultures. The birds not only get rid of the meat, their high body temperatures kill any germs they might get from cattle carcasses.

No wonder scientists were alarmed when, in 1999, biologists reported a 95 percent drop in vulture populations in India. Three vulture species — Asian white-backed, long-billed and slender-billed — were literally falling dead out of trees.

What was causing the deaths? Attention quickly turned to pesticides, heavy metals, bacteria or viruses as the possible "killer."

14

Secrets of the Dead

A huge decline in an animal population usually means an infectious epidemic is under way. The epidemic in India soon hit Nepal and Pakistan, and it could easily sweep into Africa and Europe. It was a crisis.

Many organizations stepped in to investigate, including North America's The Peregrine Fund, an organization that helps birds of prey, and the Ornithological Society of Pakistan. Scientists were sent in to do the detective work.

American microbiologist Lindsay Oaks arrived in Pakistan in 2000. A team of scientists was put together and sent out into the field to collect recently dead

Case # 5504

The Detective

Dr. Lindsay Oaks is usually found researching mammal viruses at his Washington State University lab. But as a life-long fan of falcons, eagles and other raptors and a falconer since age twelve, Oaks has worked on their conservation for years. When The Peregrine Fund asked for help, Oaks acted.

Drs. Lindsay Oaks (left) and Munir Virani

birds — a surprisingly difficult job. It was tough competing with the wild dogs for carcasses. Birds tangled in tree limbs were the collectors' best bets, unless the bodies were too old and crawling with maggots, all the clues eaten.

Vultures are not fussy about what they eat, as long as it's meat.

Scientists collected dead vultures to find out what had happened to them.

Radio satellite tags were attached to some vultures to track their movements.

Veterinarian Martin Gilbert, biologist Munir Virani and a team of graduate students did the dirty work. The more field operatives, the better the chances of finding fresh birds. In temperatures above 40°C (100°F), they hiked rough terrain, spent hours watching nests and climbed trees to pick out dead vultures.

Eventually sixteen hundred dead vultures were examined. Only 259, however, were in good enough shape to tell their story. Oaks found that 85 percent of the birds had a pasty white coating on their internal organs. The coating was uric acid, which is normally excreted by kidneys. These birds had died of kidney failure.

Only forty-five of them were fresh enough to test for the cause of kidney failure. At Oaks's lab in the United States, scientists looked for bacterial and viral infections that might have caused the kidney damage. But it soon became clear that an infection was not the killer. Whatever was killing the vultures must be a toxin — a poison. Tissue samples were sent to other labs to look for heavy metals, such as mercury, and for pesticides. Nothing.

Since most toxins are ingested (taken into the body as food), the focus turned to the vultures' diets. Vultures eat dead farm animals, and farm animals are often given veterinary drugs. Drugs are cheap and help keep an injured buffalo out in the field plowing or a goat giving milk — important if you're a small farmer and have only a few animals.

Oaks made a list of drugs used on farm animals in Pakistan, looking for a drug that specifically harms kidneys.

THE VULTURE KILLERS???
• Bad bacteria?
• Vicious viruses?
• Heavy metals?
• Pesky pesticides?

16

Pain Relief Can Be Deadly

After three years of painstaking analysis, scientists zeroed in on the culprit: a common drug used for pain relief.

Called diclofenac, the drug is similar to ibuprofen, a pain reliever found in many medicine cabinets. In India and Pakistan, farmers use diclofenac to keep injured farm animals going. Some animals die with high doses of diclofenac in their systems. When vultures eat a diclofenac-laced carcass, they die within a few days. Just one-tenth of the recommended dose for mammals is deadly to vultures. No one knew the drug was a vulture killer.

When the killer was unmasked, a meeting was organized in Kathmandu, Nepal, to ban the drug. In 2006, India was the first to outlaw the drug, and other countries followed soon after.

But more action was needed to restore the vulture population. The plan was to breed vultures in captivity, away from farm animals that have been given diclofenac. It was the only way to buy time until the vultures' usual food was safe. India began one small captive breeding program in 2004. By 2012, more than 200 vultures were in breeding programs, and more than 30 chicks had been successfully fledged.

The breeding program continues, but unfortunately diclofenac is still found in cattle. The race is on, and scientists are hoping that farm animals will be free of diclofenac in time for the vulture populations to recover.

Case # 5102

Tissue Tales

A vulture has to eat a toxic dose of diclofenac to get sick and die. If a bird just eats a little, it's fine — diclofenac isn't stored in the body. Ban the drug and the problem is solved. Some other chemicals, however, linger in the environment and in animals' bodies.

The world is full of long-lasting, human-made chemicals. Some take up residence in animals and stay there. For example, chemicals called PCBs (polychlorinated biphenyls) bind with fatty tissue in animals. PCBs can build up in the bodies of meat-eaters and pass up the food chain. Here's how it works: seals eat fish contaminated with PCBs. Then a whale eats many seals, absorbing PCBs from all of them. This is called "biomagnification," and it gets more deadly at every step up the food chain. That's why predators at the top of the food chain are especially at risk.

Chemicals build up in the fat of these seals.

Project 2: Bird Restaurant

Scientists in India tried luring vultures away from drug-filled carcasses by setting up vulture restaurants, stocked with drug-free cow carcasses. Try setting up a bird restaurant in your backyard and see what you attract. Fill it with birdseed, not dead cows.

You'll need:
- a clean milk or juice carton
- scissors
- a nail
- 2 sticks about 20 cm (8 in.) long
- string
- black oil sunflower seeds

1. Cut squares in all four sides of the carton, about halfway down. Each square should be about 8 cm (3 in.) x 8 cm (3 in.).

3. Push sticks through the holes to form a cross inside the carton. The ends should stick out to serve as perches for the birds.

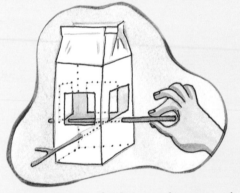

2. Use the nail to punch a small hole below each square. One set of facing holes should be slightly lower than the other.

4. Punch two holes at the top of the carton and loop the string through. Use this string to tie the feeder to a tree branch.

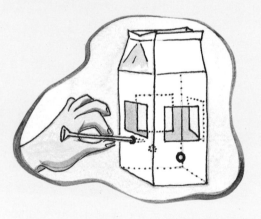

5. Fill the bottom of your feeder with seeds. What birds come to feed and when? Are they in groups or alone?

A Real Whopper

The stinky, 1.5 m (5 ft.) long fish was not welcome in the taxi. But Marjorie Courtenay Latimer insisted. She wanted to bring the fish back to the museum where she worked in East London, South Africa. Latimer often went down to the docks in search of unusual fish specimens for the museum. This one was a whopper!

A coelacanth smiles for the camera.

Back at the museum, Latimer started sifting through reference books. Her fish was strikingly similar to prehistoric fish. She made a sketch of the creature and sent it and a telegram to Rhodes University ichthyologist J.L.B. Smith. (An ichthyologist is a scientist who studies fish.) Smith, however, was away.

Latimer preserved what she could of the fish. But it's hot in South Africa, and modern preservation methods were a long way off. After three days, the fish's insides and gills were thrown out.

On January 3, 1939, Latimer received a telegram from Smith: MOST IMPORTANT PRESERVE SKELETON AND GILLS [OF] FISH DESCRIBED. Latimer searched the garbage, but the innards and gills were gone, dumped into the sea with the rest of the trash. There were no photos either. Film of the fish was inexplicably ruined.

Still, when Smith finally arrived, he identified the fish based on Latimer's drawing and description. It was a coelacanth (SEE-la-kanth), a fish thought to have been extinct for 65 million years. He named the fish *Latimeria chalumnae*, after Latimer and the area where it was found.

The Case of the Curious Corpse

The body poking out of the glacier looked like just another alpine fatality — a climber who had fallen or been caught in a storm and froze.

It was a clear day on September 19, 1991, when Erika and Helmut Simon found the body while hiking in the Alps. As they picked their way down a ridge, Helmut stopped at the strange sight: a bony, naked torso, chest down, a bald head buried in the ice. The hikers hustled to a mountain lodge and called for help.

A rescue team went to the site the next day, armed with a small jackhammer and hand tools. Freeing the body from the glacier's icy grip was tough, and the team gave up when the jackhammer gave out. It took four days of hacking at the ice to free the corpse — lots of time to notice the wood, leather and grass objects scattered around the body. Not to mention a metal axe.

The body — by now nicknamed Ötzi, or the Iceman — was shipped to a hospital in Innsbruck, Austria. Ötzi and the mysterious objects found along side him were

examined by a local archaeologist (a scientist who studies past human cultures). One look at the small axe and flint dagger and he knew: this was no unlucky twentieth-century hiker.

Reading the Remains

The axe was the biggest clue to Ötzi's age — it was at least four thousand years old. The axe was similar to others from that time period, and the metal looked like bronze. Its presence suggested that Ötzi was an ice mummy from long ago.

The archaeology detectives swung into gear. Grass samples were sent to experts for radiocarbon dating, and Ötzi was packed in crushed ice and stored in a refrigerated vault to preserve him. Meanwhile scientists went back to scour the gully where he was found for more clues.

In early December, radiocarbon dating knocked the socks off the archaeologists. Ötzi was actually fifty-three hundred years old. He was a human time capsule from the Copper Age, an era that stretched from six thousand to four thousand years ago.

The jackhammer, unfortunately, had cracked the time capsule, tearing flesh from the mummy's left hip and damaging the thigh bone. Rough handling had also damaged Ötzi's gear. His long bow was broken and his backpack frame was in pieces. Was it worn over the head or shoulder? We'll probably never know.

This is Ötzi (rhymes with Tootsie). Even his eyes were preserved by his icy tomb.

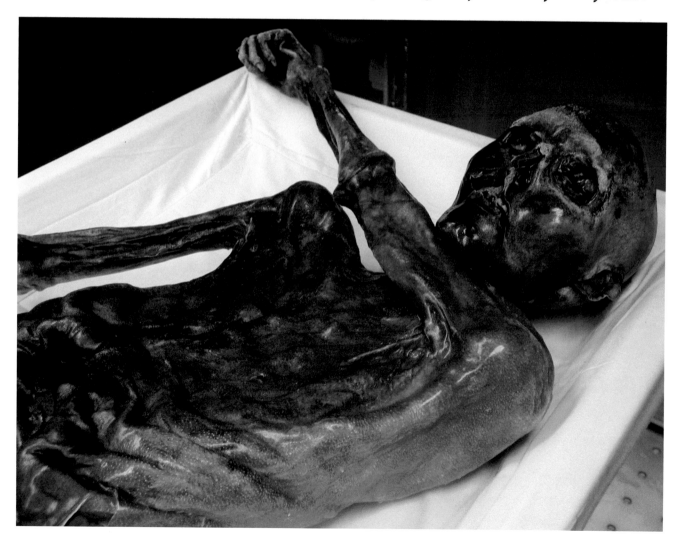

The first rounds of testing revealed that the 1.6 m (5 ft. 3 in.) tall Iceman's age was about forty-six. Tiny bits of material from Ötzi's gut went to Austrian botanist Klaus Oeggl. He found evidence of the Iceman's last meal — bread made from einkorn, a primitive wheat farmed by ancient people. Ah ha! Ötzi had had contact with an agricultural community.

An electron microscope revealed even more. Oeggl turned up partially digested plants, meat, whipworm and tree pollen. Analyses of the layers of soil from the area showed that the tree from which the pollen came (hop hornbeam) at that time grew down in the valley, a five- or six-hour walk from Ötzi's final resting place. The tree blooms in late spring. So Ötzi had traveled in late spring, climbing into the snowy mountains from a valley below.

He was dressed for the weather at least. A grass cape kept Ötzi warm, along with a knee-length goatskin coat, leggings, a loincloth and a bearskin cap. A calf-leather belt held tools and supplies. Ötzi's grass-stuffed shoes had bearskin soles and deerskin uppers. By washing residues from Ötzi's clothes, scientists found a moss that grew south of the mountain pass, confirming the Iceman's whereabouts before his alpine climb.

His supplies showed him to be a self-sufficient hiker and hunter. They included birchbark containers, a net made from grass, the backpack, a deerskin quiver with fourteen arrows and the very useful axe, which turned out to be made from copper, not bronze. Reconstructing the tools told them more. Two arrows, though broken, revealed an understanding of flight — each had three feathers for stability, just like those on modern-day arrows.

Scientists thought that was the end of Ötzi's story. Then, in 1998, Ötzi was moved to the South Tyrol Museum of Archaeology in Bolzano, Italy. An old bank building had been converted to a museum, with a high-tech refrigerated vault already tested on other mummies.

The Murdered Mummy

In a chilled chamber that mimics Ötzi's snowy grave, pathologist Dr. Eduard Egarter Vigl simply kept the mummy well preserved for the first couple of years. Little did he suspect that more secrets could be drawn from the Iceman.

Then an Austrian researcher asked him to take more x-rays of Ötzi's broken ribs. The x-rays revealed no broken ribs — the original researcher had mistaken two overlapping ribs for a fracture. Further x-rays and scans by the Italian team showed a dark, triangular shape embedded in Ötzi's left shoulder. By examining it, Egarter Vigl

could tell it was an entry wound caused by an arrow — the Iceman had been shot from behind. Also, judging from its depth — the point had just missed a lung — the arrow was probably launched from more than 60 m (200 ft.) away.

Ötzi didn't die immediately though. And he had company — someone had pulled out the arrow's shaft. The nature of the wound told researchers Ötzi was in pain. The main nerve of the left arm was cut, probably causing paralysis. And there was one last discovery. Ötzi may have fought his attacker. A documentary filmmaker tipped Egarter Vigl off to that clue.

Case # 3930

The Detective

Before Ötzi blew into Bolzano, Italy, Dr. Eduard Egarter Vigl headed the pathology department at the local hospital. When someone was murdered, he would be involved with the autopsy. And yet this scientist had wanted to be a truck driver when he was a kid.

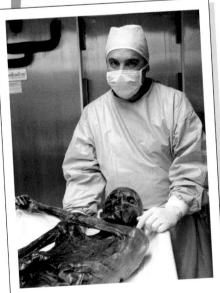

Dr. Egarter Vigl with his charge, Ötzi.

As a surgical and forensic pathologist, Egarter Vigl teased out the secrets of the human body after death. He worked daily with police to solve crimes. It was Ötzi who steered him to more ancient mysteries.

Not only did the pathologist reveal Ötzi's fatal encounter, but he and his staff keep the Iceman in mint mummy condition, so that he can answer further questions.

While workers were extracting Ötzi from the ice, someone noticed an object clenched in the Iceman's right hand. It was picked up and thrown aside. A film made at the time shows the toss, and then the camera zooms in on the object — a flint dagger. So Ötzi was shot with an arrow and died holding a dagger. Egarter Vigl thawed Ötzi's right hand and found a deep, jagged cut across the palm and another cut on his wrist. Hand-to-hand combat? Maybe.

More research a few years later coaxed the answer and other secrets from the Iceman. DNA analysis revealed that Ötzi was lactose intolerant (no milk for him) and had brown eyes and type O blood. The analysis also told scientists that he was prone to heart disease. The DNA from his full belly revealed that Ötzi had eaten wild goat not long before he died. And using nanotechnology to study the blood from the mummy's wound, researchers discovered how long Ötzi had lived after being shot with the arrow — thirty minutes at most. A protein, fibrin, was detected in his blood. After being wounded, the body releases fibrin to help the blood clot. As a wound heals, fibrin dissipates. If there was a fight, it was brief.

Case # 2311

Peering Inside Bones

Archaeologists are sometimes faced with a dilemma: how to unravel a mystery without destroying the evidence. Thanks to modern medicine they can peer into mummies using tools that barely leave a mark.

X-rays are commonly used. Ötzi was x-rayed, as were his artifacts. A pouch found near him was x-rayed before scientists withdrew the three flint tools it contained.

In CAT (computerized axial tomography) scans, a beam of x-rays moves around the body in a circle to give better details, especially of the chest and belly areas. Images are processed by a computer and can give a three-dimensional portrait of a body. CAT scans revealed the arrowhead embedded in Ötzi's back.

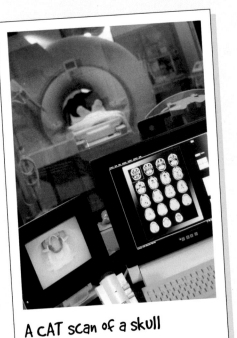
A CAT scan of a skull

The Littlest Humans

In September 2003, archaeologists were wrapping up a dig in Liang Bua Cave on the Indonesian island of Flores. One of their last finds was unusual — a nearly complete, child-sized skeleton. They labeled it Liang Bua 1, or LB1.

The bones were sent to the lab, where Australian scientist Dr. Peter Brown examined LB1. What he found gave him quite a shock — LB1 had lived eighteen thousand years ago, died around age thirty and is an entirely new species of human: *Homo floresiensis*. Scientists call this tiny human the original hobbit.

H. floresiensis stood about 1 m (3 ft.) tall and had a small brain — the smallest of any human species. The average modern human brain is 1400 cubic cm (85 cubic in.), about three times the size of LB1's grapefruit-sized brain, 380 cubic cm (23 cubic in.). The discovery that LB1 is a new hominin (human relative) has shaken the human family tree.

The remains of six other individuals — yes, they're small too — were also found, along with stone tools and the remains of dwarf elephants called Stegodon. Cutmarks on the elephant bones suggest that *H. floresiensis* hunted and butchered the Stegodon.

So, scientists found small humans, small Stegodon and stone tools sophisticated enough to carve up an elephant. All this during a time period thought to be populated by only us, *Homo sapiens*. Turns out we had other human company, on Flores Island at least.

This is where the child-sized skeleton was found.

Bones told scientists a lot about the hobbit-like humans.

Project 3: Frozen Finds

To keep Ötzi preserved, scientists had to keep him in the same condition as the glacier he was found in: frozen. His artifacts (tools, clothing and so on), however, were thawed and studied. How does freezing and thawing affect artifacts? Try this and see.

You'll need:
- 5 plastic cups
- shreds of newspaper
- small pieces of bread
- 3 berries
- a small nail
- a metal paper clip
- a green leaf
- some grass
- a leather shoelace
- small rocks
- tweezers
- a pencil
- a sheet of paper

1. Put newspaper in one cup, bread and berries in another cup, the nail and paper clip in another cup, the leaf in the fourth cup and the grass and shoelace in the last cup.

2. Fill each cup three-quarters full with water and place rocks on top of the "artifacts" to weigh them down. Freeze the cups.

3. After three days, let the cups thaw. Remove the "artifacts" with the tweezers. Write down the condition of each object. Have they changed?

4. Place the artifacts in a dry, bright place. After another four days, look at them again. How do they look now? Is an artifact affected by the way it is stored?

On the Viking Trail

Norse sagas tell riveting tales of Viking Leif Eriksson sailing from Greenland to establish a colony in a place they called Vinland around the year 1000. But were the stories fact or fiction?

Fiction, said most people. A map of Vinland found in 1440 was considered a fake. But a handful of detectives over the centuries persisted in uncovering the truth. An unlikely detective, eighteenth-century sea captain James Cook, also a famous mapmaker, deduced that Vinland was what is now northeastern Newfoundland.

Around 1913, Newfoundlander William Munn read the sagas looking for other hints — sailing directions, landfall descriptions and dates. He narrowed the location of Leif's arrival to L'Anse aux Meadows in Newfoundland's northern peninsula. But Munn lacked hard evidence. An American navy captain explored the area and turned up iron nails and Viking boat rivets but no ruins.

It took a Viking descendant to solve the mystery. Norwegian Helge Ingstad followed a hunch and an Icelandic map when he launched his search in 1960. He landed in a Newfoundland fishing village where he asked a local fisherman if any ruins were close by. The fisherman pointed the way to what the locals thought were Aboriginal burial mounds. The mounds turned out to be the ruins of Viking sod houses.

Ingstad returned with his archaeologist wife, Anne Stine, and a research team. Eight summers of digging revealed indisputable evidence of Vikings — homes, a blacksmith shop, soapstone oil lamps, bone needles and more iron nails.

The remains of sod houses (now reconstructed) are solid evidence that Vikings lived at L'Anse aux Meadows.

The Case of the Hot Ice

There's plenty of ice in the Northwest Territories, but it's not all frozen water. Some of it is rock hard, diamond hard. It's hot ice — diamonds.

Not that diamonds were just lying around in the open waiting to be discovered. It took a super sleuth and a decade of searching to find the diamonds in Canada's north. Geologist Charles (Chuck) Fipke used science, technology and persistence to turn a dream of finding diamonds into one of the biggest mining success stories of the twentieth century. Diamonds in Canada? You bet — $2.8 billion worth so far.

Case # 8327

Diamond Detective

Name: Charles (Chuck) Fipke
Born: July 22, 1946
Nickname: Captain Chaos
Education: B.Sc. (Honors) Geology, University of British Columbia (1970)
Hobby: Horse breeding

Charles Fipke

A Crack in the Case

Charles Fipke had worked with geologists in South Africa, the world's largest diamond-producing country, and had learned a few of the tricks to finding diamonds. Now he turned his know-how to North America.

The first "trick" was to find kimberlite pipes. These volcanic veins are the routes through which diamonds rise from deep underground to Earth's surface. Diamonds are formed more than 120 km (70 mi.) below ground. There, under great pressure and extremely high temperatures, simple carbon atoms are transformed into stellar diamonds.

The diamonds are brought up to the surface when molten rock (magma) spurts upwards and erupts through Earth's crust. This upward tunneling magma becomes a long tube, or "pipe," of kimberlite (rocks and big crystals glued together by the magma as it cools). Fipke was looking for the tops of these kimberlite pipes.

When magma erupts at the surface, a crater is formed, which should make finding a pipe easy. Just look for a crater and start digging. But the craters are often covered by layers of rock and debris, and sometimes they fill with water. That's why finding them is tricky.

The Fab Four

So how do you find kimberlite pipes if they're hidden from sight? One good way is to look for much more abundant "indicator minerals," such

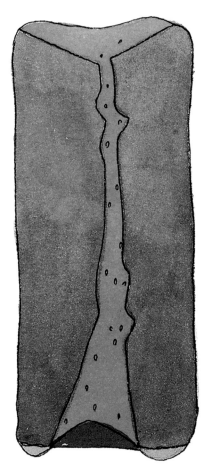

Magma gushes up through rock, carrying diamonds with it and forming a pipe. A crater is formed at the surface.

as olivine, ilmenite, garnet and chrome diopside. These minerals often indicate the presence nearby of diamond-carrying kimberlite pipes.

Minerals change with certain pressures and temperatures. Chrome diopside, for example, needs high temperatures to form. Finding this mineral would tell Fipke if the temperature was high enough for diamonds to form, too.

Fipke also knew that no two pipes have the same ilmenites. If he collected different ilmenites, it probably meant there was more than one pipe in the area and therefore better odds of finding diamonds. And Fipke knew that a specific garnet, called G10, was a mineral to look for if you wanted to find diamonds. The two often went together.

Fipke began his search in the Rocky Mountains near Golden, British Columbia, in 1979. After finding some chrome diopside, he called in his buddy, Stewart Blusson, a geologist with twenty years' experience working for the Geological Survey of Canada.

With Blusson at the controls of an ancient helicopter, the pair discovered twenty-six kimberlite pipes poking out of bare limestone rock in one crazy day. Although the pipes didn't carry the sparkling gem, the friends were struck with "diamond fever."

But there were still a few obstacles to overcome. How do you raise money to look for diamonds without letting the competition know what you're up to? And how do you keep tabs on what other prospectors are doing? Big ears and even bigger eyes — all the better to keep track of the competition. Three years after their British Columbia expedition, Fipke and Blusson learned that the giant diamond company DeBeers was looking for diamonds in the Northwest Territories. Fipke and Blusson high-tailed it north, too.

Through winter deep freezes and bug-infested summers, the two diamond-hunters continued their search. Then, success! Fipke found indicator minerals. But there was a problem. Glaciers. These icy flows had slid over the area,

carrying the mineral clues with them and depositing them far from their original location. Where exactly were the kimberlite pipes that they had come from?

Fipke and Blusson followed the path that the glacier had taken, collecting mineral samples as they went. Like Hansel and Gretel, they tracked the trail of "crumbs" until it went cold. The samples were sent back to Fipke's lab for analysis. Fipke had a special and secret way of looking for one indicator

Case # 3505

Multi-faceted

Diamonds from Africa, the largest source of diamonds in the world, are often traded illegally to fund brutal civil wars. Angola, Sierra Leone and the Democratic Republic of the Congo have all suffered as a result. Called "blood" diamonds, these stones make up 20 percent of the global rough diamond trade ("rough" is what the diamonds are called before they are cut and polished). Diamonds from Canada, on the other hand, are "conflict free." To help end the blood-diamond trade, there is an international system of recording and tracking diamonds from the mines to the jewelers.

Glaciers can carry minerals far away from their original locations.

dark — he told them they were searching for gold.

As sample after sample was tested, Fipke became increasingly excited. And then he found the kimberlite pipe. It was under a lake. He rushed to stake claims. One kimberlite pipe was drilled to a depth of 290 m (950 ft.), and a 59 kg (130 lb.) sample was collected.

In the lab Fipke washed away the soils, separated light minerals from heavy and put the tray of heavy minerals under an electron microscope. There, glinting like ice, with no kimberlite left to hide their brilliance, were diamonds — eighty-one diamonds. The diamond rush in Canada's north was about to begin.

This is kimberlite.

mineral, G10 garnet. And it worked. He found G10 in some of the rock samples. And he knew where those samples had come from.

They were from an area 300 km (185 mi.) northeast of Yellowknife, near Lac de Gras. Fipke was sure the G10s would lead them to a pipe holding the diamonds.

The team sampled feverishly, collecting bag after bag of rocks and sending them to the lab, where they were studied carefully under a scanning electron microscope.

Shhh! It's a Secret

The searching and the sampling were done with great secrecy. After all, anyone could come along at any moment and stake a claim in the area that would allow them sole access to the minerals it held. Fipke even kept his crew in the

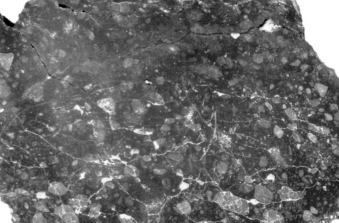

Precious Price Tag

Diamonds are measured in metric carats. The word "carat" comes from the name of a seed once used as a measure of weight. One carat equals 0.2 g (0.007 oz.). A kimberlite pipe is mined for diamonds if it has at least half a carat per ton of rock. That's like finding a tick (with a full belly) on an African elephant.

Of all diamonds mined, only 20 percent are good enough to become gemstones for jewelry. The remaining 80 percent are used for industrial purposes, such as metal-cutting tools, rock drills and grinding wheels. Diamonds, after all, are the hardest minerals on Earth, which means they stay sharp longer.

Project 4: Oh Moh!

Identifying minerals is a science. Geologists examine the form of the crystal (most minerals occur naturally as crystals) for its hardness, color and cleavage (how it splits apart) and measure its specific gravity (its weight in relation to an equal volume of water).

Here's a simple experiment to determine hardness. Find a rock sample. According to the Mohs Scale of Hardness (developed in 1812 in Austria by mineralogist Friedrich Mohs), if the rock can be scratched by your fingernail, it has a hardness of less than 2.5. Try scratching it with a penny (hardness 3), a pocket-knife blade (5.5) and a steel file (6.5). (Important: get an adult to help you with the knife and file.) Talc (think baby powder) has a hardness of 1. Diamonds top the scale at 10. Where does your rock fit in?

Unsolved Mystery of the Rolling Stones

Racetrack Playa is an old, dried-up lake bed in Death Valley, California, that is littered with rocks. Some are as small as your fist; others are as big as picnic coolers. This is where it starts to get weird. The rocks move, leaving behind tracks as evidence. What's making them move? Geologists have tried to figure it out. They have documented the tracks, the size of stones and even named the rocks. But so far, they've had no luck in solving the mystery.

In 1948, geologists from the United States Geological Survey suggested that dust devils — mini-tornadoes — twirled the rocks across the landscape. But there was no proof. In 1955, geologist George Stanley theorized that the rocks moved when ice sheets formed on the playa surface after a flood. Well, plausible. Racetrack Playa is 1130 m (3708 ft.) above sea level, and the temperature can drop to below freezing. And water sometimes floods the playa. But no one had ever witnessed ice on the playa. In fact, no one had ever witnessed the rocks moving.

Two other geologists began a study in 1968. They measured the positions of thirty rocks and put stakes around some of them. Each year they checked back and noted that some rocks had moved, while others had not. They gave up in 1975.

More studies followed. In 2001, geologist Paula Messina took GPS (Global Positioning System) measurements of all rocks before they moved and after. Her conclusion? She found that the rocks move in any direction they please with no rhyme or reason. Messina believes the playa gets slick with mud, and when strong winds blow, the rocks move. Other geologists accept the wind idea, but think ice still might play a part in the movement.

Until someone sees the rocks roll (or slide), the mystery remains.

This rock is on a roll.

The Case of the Twisted Code

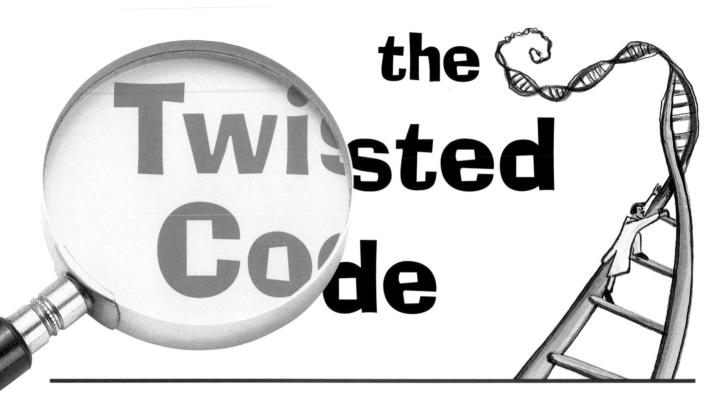

It was a long and winding road that led to the detection of DNA, the stuff that makes you you, and everyone else, well, everyone else.

Coiled inside almost every cell in your body is a long molecule called deoxyribonucleic acid (DNA). (A molecule consists of two or more atoms bonded together.)

DNA contains the instructions — scientists call them "genes" — for all living things. For example, if your eyes are brown it's because your genes gave instructions for brown eyes.

It's the same for curly hair, straight hair, red hair or brown hair.

And yet this very important stuff is quite ordinary to look at. If you isolated

some of your DNA in a test tube and pulled it out with tweezers, it would look just like threads of gooey cotton. Or snot. How do we know about DNA and how it works?

The Inheritance

For thousands of years parents knew that if one of them had red hair, there was a good chance some of their children would, too. And if mom and dad had brown eyes? A brown-eyed baby was expected, although occasionally grandma's or grandpa's blue eyes showed up. Common sense told people that physical characteristics, such as eye color or height, could be passed from one generation to the next.

Farmers used this knowledge to improve their crops or livestock. A farmer with a cow that was a super milk producer would breed the cow to produce calves that would also grow up to be good milkers.

But how *exactly* did instructions on eye color and milk production and so on get passed along? That was the mystery.

At first, people believed blood was the key to inherited characteristics. Then one nineteenth-century researcher proved that theory was wrong. He took blood from a black rabbit and gave it to a white rabbit in a blood

transfusion. When the white rabbit had little rabbits, they were ... white. So much for the blood theory.

Notice any similar physical traits in this family?

It took an Austrian monk with a lot of time and a lot of pea plants to set things straight. In the 1860s, Gregor Mendel bred garden peas to show that traits (physical characteristics) were passed to the next generation through some hidden mechanism *within* the plant. He had no idea what that was, but his study was a new and important clue to the mystery.

Case # 5504

Playing with His Peas

For eight years Austrian monk Gregor Mendel took detailed notes of twenty-eight thousand pea plants he grew. Mendel was examining seven pea plant traits, each of which came in two forms, such as color (pods of a pea plant are either green or yellow), seed texture (round or wrinkled) and height (tall or dwarfed). To see what happened when, for instance, a tall plant was crossbred with a short one, he brushed the pollen of one pea plant onto the pistils of another to create all-new, never-before-seen plants, called hybrids.

When these hybrids in turn produced offspring, he noted how many plants were tall, how many were short. At the time most people assumed inheritance was blended — tall plus short should come out medium. But Mendel's plants were either tall or short (or green or yellow, or their seeds round or wrinkled). His work proved that individual traits were physically passed from generation to generation and also that some traits were dominant over others. For example, in Labrador retrievers, black fur is dominant over yellow fur.

When Mendel was through, he handed biologists a breakthrough in genetics.

Around the same time, a curious Swiss doctor began collecting pus-soaked bandages from a local hospital. Pus has lots of white blood cells, which are large and perfect for studying the cell's control center, the nucleus. The doctor identified an acid compound found in the nucleus and nowhere else in a cell. He called it nucleic acid.

For the next forty years, scientists found out more and more about cells. They studied how cells divide, they found egg cells, sperm cells, proteins, chromosomes (coiled, string-like parts of a cell nucleus) — you name it. But they still didn't know how a cell got instructions, for example, to make a flower red rather than blue, or how a parent passed along genetic information to a child.

Fast forward to 1904 and the humble fruit fly. One fruit fly couple produces three generations and three million flies in a month — ideal for studying inheritance. A scientist named Thomas Hunt Morgan noted that fruit flies passed on physical traits just as Mendel's pea plants did, except for one thing: sex made a difference. For example, in flies, eye color is passed on by the female. The chromosomes in the nucleus of the cell seemed to hold the secret of why this happened.

Code Breakers

A chromosome consists of coils of DNA wrapped around proteins. At first scientists thought these proteins were responsible for physical traits. But in 1944 scientists cross-breeding two types of pneumonia bacteria found that DNA, not the proteins, passed along inheritance information. All attention shifted to DNA.

DNA is made up of four chemicals: adenine (A), guanine (G), thymine (T) and cytosine (C). Scientists began to suspect that the arrangement of these chemicals was like a

code that could send instructions to cells. They felt the code must somehow involve the shape of DNA molecules.

Several scientists began to work on cracking the DNA code. Enter Francis Crick and James Watson. Crick was a physicist and Watson was a biologist. That was a handicap. Neither had much chemistry knowledge, which was essential to analyzing the shape of DNA and how the code worked. But that didn't stop them. In the 1950s, the pair read chemistry books and picked the brains of leading chemists, some of whom laughed at their weak understanding of chemistry.

While Crick and Watson worked away at England's Cambridge University, Rosalind Franklin and Maurice Wilkins were nearby in London at King's College using x-ray cameras to photograph DNA molecules.

In November 1951, Franklin gave a talk on her research. Watson traveled to London to attend. He reported back to Crick, who promptly sketched a possible DNA molecule based on what Watson had told him.

Watson (left) and Crick (right) look at their DNA model.

Crick and Watson decided to build a model of DNA using metal plates and rods. When they were finished, they invited Franklin and Wilkins to see the structure. Just one small problem. It seems Watson hadn't quite understood Franklin's talk. The model was wrong.

Crick and Watson were told by their supervisor to stop working on DNA and get back to their usual research. But they wouldn't give up. The real breakthrough came when Wilkins showed them Rosalind Franklin's clearest-ever x-ray photograph of a DNA molecule, Photo 51.

Photo 51 showed that DNA had a distinctive cross shape. Crick and Watson used geometry to work out that the cross shape was actually part of a twisting ladder, which they called a double helix.

They had the shape. And they also had an idea that the chemicals — A, G, T and C — formed the rungs of the ladder. Each rung, they said, is made up of two chemicals (A and T or G and C) bonded together. The order of these

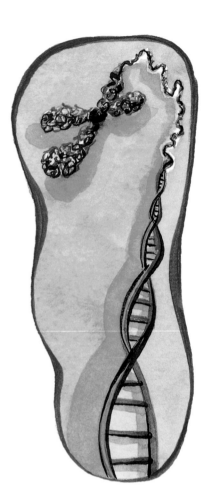

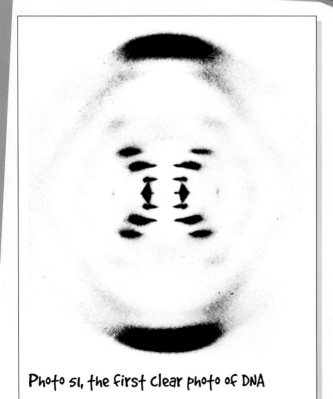

Case # 2109

Photo 51, the first clear photo of DNA

Photo 51: A picture worth a thousand words

Without Photo 51, Francis Crick and James Watson could have lost the race to decipher DNA. The technique used to capture the picture was x-ray crystallography. It sprays molecules with x-rays, which bend and spread in a certain pattern when they hit the molecules. The pattern was captured on film in 1952 by Rosalind Franklin. Applying math to the pattern lets scientists build a three-dimensional model of how atoms are arranged on a molecule.

Dynamic DNA Duo

An overpowering laugh would announce that Francis Crick was in the room. The thirty-five-year-old British physicist — still pursuing his doctorate — seemed an unlikely candidate to discover the secret of life. James Watson was a biologist who studied birds.

A few years before they met, both men had read famous physicist Erwin Schrödinger's influential science book, *What Is Life?* Schrödinger wrote that chromosomes carry information in code and to crack the code was to understand life.

Crick and Watson were hooked. Crick wandered into the mysteries of chemistry and biology, and Watson abandoned birds for viruses and then DNA. When they met at Cambridge University, they hit it off instantly. And so began a collaboration that unlocked the mystery of life.

The human body has about 100 trillion cells. The DNA in a single cell, if all 23 pairs of chromosomes were stretched out end to end, is about 1.8 m (6 ft.) long. Red blood cells do not have DNA.

chemical pairs determines physical traits. It was now early in 1953, and Crick and Watson quickly built a cardboard model of the DNA molecule. This time it was right.

In 1909, Danish botanist Wilhelm Johannsen called the still unknown "things" that passed on information from one living thing to another, genes. It's from the Greek word "genea," meaning generation.

By solving the mystery of DNA's shape, this daring duo figured out how genetic traits were passed from one generation to the next. The structure of the ladder itself passes on these traits. Imagine you had a ladder and you took a saw and cut it in half lengthwise. With a bit of work, you could make two ladders out of the one by adding on to the half ladders. You'd only need one side of the ladder to know how to build the missing side to make a new one.

It's the same with DNA. Only, instead of building a new ladder, you'd be building a new cell nucleus that is a copy of the old one. This is how your genes pass along information to new cells as your body grows. (*Keep making red hair, you hair cells!*)

How are genetic traits passed from parents to child? Each parent takes half a ladder, makes a new whole one and passes it onto their kids. So you have one ladder (actually a set of chromosomes) from your father and one from your mother.

Because your parents pass on slightly different sets of chromosomes to each of their children, you share some, but not all, genetic traits with your brothers and sisters. You may have red hair, while your brother's is blond.

Today, fifty years later,

scientists have produced a map of the position and order of human genes called the Human Genome, as well as maps for some plants, animals, bacteria and viruses. But they realized it's like having the parts list for an airplane, yet still not knowing how to build the airplane or make it fly. The next step in the mystery goes almost back to the beginning: proteins. DNA is like a cookbook, filled with protein recipes. The cell is the cook in the kitchen. Even when it has the right recipes, the cell still has the hard work of cooking up the different proteins that make you — hair, skin, hormones, everything.

Nevertheless, a parts list is pretty impressive.

Case # 5405

The Dark Lady

Things were so unfriendly at Rosalind Franklin's lab that the men started calling her "the dark lady." In fact, Franklin was an intelligent, independent and meticulous scientist. Cambridge, however, was a man's domain. Women scientists could not even eat lunch in the common room where the men ate.

At age fifteen, Franklin knew that science was her life's calling. Cambridge University gave her a scholarship, and by her twenties she was a well-established scientist, working on coal. (Her work launched the field of high-tech carbon fibers used in bicycles, spacecraft and boats.) But x-ray diffraction images intrigued her.

Franklin's interest switched to creating images of crystallized solids, such as coal, using x-ray cameras. Franklin was good at it, and she moved back to Cambridge University from Paris to photograph DNA. The move would change genetics forever after she snapped the legendary Photo 51.

Franklin eventually left Cambridge and began research on viruses. Some researchers believe her x-ray work led to the cancer that killed her, at the age of thirty-seven, in 1958. Back then

Rosalind Franklin

researchers did not wear lead aprons to protect them from x-ray radiation.

While Crick and Watson won a Nobel Prize in 1962 for their work in cracking the DNA code, Rosalind Franklin's important contribution is only now being recognized.

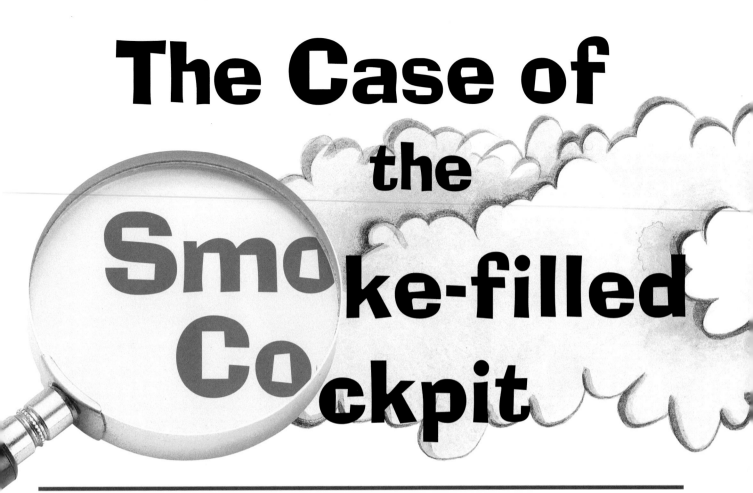

The Case of the Smoke-filled Cockpit

"Pan! Pan! Pan!" Dinner was being served to the 215 passengers aboard Swissair Flight 111 when Captain Urs Zimmerman made the call — a universal signal that there was a problem on board.

The wide-body jet, a Boeing MD-11, was only fifty-three minutes into its flight from JFK Airport in New York en route to Geneva, Switzerland, when Captain Zimmerman and First Officer Stephan Loew smelled smoke in the cockpit. Checking it out, they thought there was a problem with the air conditioning system. Air traffic control suggested landing at the airport in nearby Halifax, Nova Scotia. Pilot and first officer agreed.

Donning their oxygen masks, the pilots began descending from a cruising altitude of 9500 m (31 000 ft.). They were 56 km (34.5 mi.) from the end of the runway. The pilots said they needed more distance to lose altitude and dump excess fuel for a safer landing. Nothing more was heard from Swissair Flight 111.

Black Void

When Swissair Flight 111 crashed into the ocean near Peggy's Cove, Nova Scotia, on September 2, 1998, accident investigators were faced with a mystery. Why did the plane crash? Why was there smoke in the cockpit?

Engineers looked at what clues they had. Weather

was first. An offshore hurricane could have been a factor. That was quickly ruled out. Another big clue was the plane itself. A year earlier, a major overhaul had been done, and the plane had been literally taken apart and put back together. Could there have been a mechanical problem? The other clues were human. What did the pilots say and do?

There were no survivors of Swissair 111. All 229 passengers and crew perished. With no one to tell the story, it was crucial to find as many pieces of the plane as possible in order to reconstruct what had happened.

Swissair 111 went down near the tiny fishing village of Peggy's Cove, Nova Scotia.

Case # 8245

Last Words

Halifax Air Traffic Control: *Swissair one eleven just a couple of miles I'll be right with you.*

Swissair 111: *Roger. [sound of autopilot being disconnected] And we are declaring emergency now, Swissair one eleven.*

Halifax ATC: *Copy that. Swissair one eleven you are cleared to, ah, commence your fuel dump on that track and advise me, ah, when the dump is complete.*

Swissair 111: *[unintelligible]*

— Captain Urs Zimmermann and First Officer Stephan Loew, Swissair 111, last recorded words before crashing off the coast of Nova Scotia, September 2, 1998

SWISSAIR III SUSPECTS
• Howling hurricane?
• Mechanical meltdown?
• Pilot problems?
• Fatal fire?

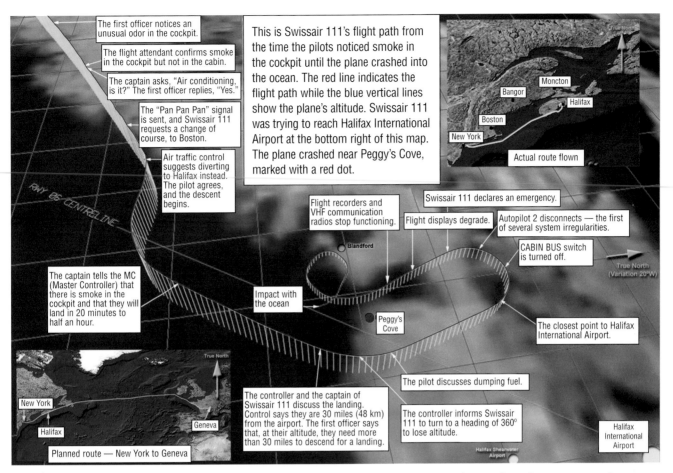

The first officer notices an unusual odor in the cockpit.

The flight attendant confirms smoke in the cockpit but not in the cabin.

The captain asks, "Air conditioning, is it?" The first officer replies, "Yes."

The "Pan Pan Pan" signal is sent, and Swissair 111 requests a change of course, to Boston.

Air traffic control suggests diverting to Halifax instead. The pilot agrees, and the descent begins.

This is Swissair 111's flight path from the time the pilots noticed smoke in the cockpit until the plane crashed into the ocean. The red line indicates the flight path while the blue vertical lines show the plane's altitude. Swissair 111 was trying to reach Halifax International Airport at the bottom right of this map. The plane crashed near Peggy's Cove, marked with a red dot.

Moncton

Bangor

Halifax

Boston

New York

Actual route flown

Swissair 111 declares an emergency.

Flight displays degrade.

Autopilot 2 disconnects — the first of several system irregularities.

Flight recorders and VHF communication radios stop functioning.

CABIN BUS switch is turned off.

True North (Variation 20°W)

Blandford

The captain tells the MC (Master Controller) that there is smoke in the cockpit and that they will land in 20 minutes to half an hour.

Impact with the ocean

Peggy's Cove

The closest point to Halifax International Airport.

RWY 06 CENTRELINE

True North

New York

Halifax

Geneva

Planned route — New York to Geneva

The controller and the captain of Swissair 111 discuss the landing. Control says they are 30 miles (48 km) from the airport. The first officer says that, at their altitude, they need more than 30 miles to descend for a landing.

The pilot discusses dumping fuel.

The controller informs Swissair 111 to turn to a heading of 360° to lose altitude.

Halifax Shearwater Airport

Halifax International Airport

The plane was traveling at about 550 km/h (350 m.p.h.) when it hit the water. It was torn apart on impact, with pieces landing deep underwater and 9 km (6 mi.) off the coast.

It took almost a week to find what investigators hoped to be a crucial clue: the "black box" that is supposed to record everything said in the cockpit. Divers grabbed Swissair 111's cockpit voice recorder off the ocean floor 55 m (180 ft.) below the icy waves. But electricity had been shut off during the last six minutes of the flight. The voice recorder yielded no clues.

The wreckage was all investigators had to work with. Floating debris was quickly picked up off the surface of the water.

Along the cove's rocky shore is a memorial to the 229 crash victims.

IN MEMORY OF
THE 229 MEN WOMEN AND CHILDREN
ABOARD SWISSAIR FLIGHT 111
WHO PERISHED OFF THESE SHORES
SEPTEMBER 2, 1998

THEY HAVE BEEN JOINED TO THE
SEA AND THE SKY

MAY THEY REST IN PEACE

A LA MÉMOIRE
DES 229 HOMMES, FEMMES ET ENFANTS
QUI ONT PERDU LA VIE AU LARGE DE
CES CÔTES VOL SWISSAIR 111
LE 2 SEPTEMBRE 1998

ILS APPARTIENNENT MAINTENANT
AU CIEL ET À LA MER

QU'ILS REPOSENT EN PAIX

Scattered by wind and wave action, bits and pieces were collected along the shoreline. Divers went looking for the underwater pieces. Cranes, boats and ROVs (remotely operated vehicles) combed the area. And, finally, the area was dredged (dug up) four times, with 1.5 m (5 ft.) of mud and debris sucked off the ocean floor.

Even super-small pieces of wire were crucial to the investigation. The plane contained no less than 250 km (155 mi.) of wire. Most of it was torn apart into finger- to arm-length pieces. Investigators labeled, recorded and boxed every single bit of wreckage found, including the tiny bits of wire.

Puzzle Masters

While technicians labored to collect the wreckage, researchers interviewed eyewitnesses who had seen the plane before it plunged into the ocean. From flight transcripts,

they knew there was smoke in the cockpit. One witness saw a glow at the front of the left wing. Another saw a smoky haze following the aircraft. But no one reported seeing fire. The passengers and crew died when the plane hit the water. One of them was even wearing a life jacket, which suggests that they had some warning.

The pieces of recovered plane were the last hope for solving the mystery. As contorted chunks of metal were identified, they were straightened and sorted. A full-scale model of the front 10 m (33 ft.) of the plane was assembled like a jigsaw puzzle. Expert technicians used the plane's manufacturing drawings to help them place the pieces correctly.

The focus was on the smoke. The pilots had done everything right, including going through a long checklist of why smoke might be filling the cockpit. Investigators found the reason within a few weeks of assembling the model: fire above the ceiling in the rear of the cockpit. But how did the fire start?

The best guess was the wiring. Electrical fires are fast and ferocious. On Swissair 111, the cockpit wires and electronics were

The Black Box

Something eavesdrops on commercial pilots as they fly. It's known as the "black box," though it's really bright orange so it will be easier to find after an accident. The box can hold both the flight data recorder (FDR) and the cockpit voice recorder (CVR), or each can be in its own box, housed in the tail of the plane. These recorders give investigators hints of where to start in their search for clues after a crash.

The container itself is tough. It must withstand a force 3400 times the force of gravity and be unaffected by flames raging for thirty minutes. A crash into an ocean is no problem either — the box can survive submersion at 600 m (1970 ft.) for thirty days. Either heat-treated stainless steel or titanium makes the box almost indestructible.

The CVR picks up the conversation between the flight crew and listens for other noises, such as switches being turned on or off. It records in a continuous thirty-minute loop, dumping the oldest recording as new information is added. The FDR monitors information from the plane — airspeed, altitude, direction, time, flap position and so on — and can log up to twenty-five hours of information.

While news reports often focus on what the pilots said before a crash, the data recorder is sometimes more important. The data recorder provides the information needed to create a computer-animated, video reconstruction of the flight. In the case of Swissair 111, however, the last six minutes of both the CVR and FDR were missing.

Today, black boxes must hold two hours of cockpit sound and have back-up batteries in case the plane's electrical system fails. It was an electrical system malfunction that silenced Swissair 111's black boxes.

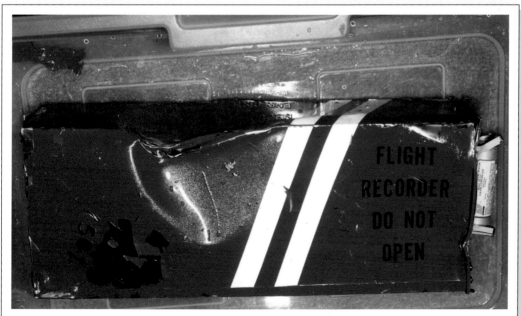

The first black box was found four days after the crash, the second box ten days after the crash.

seriously heat-damaged, indicating that this was where the fire burned longest. Using computer simulations and laboratory tests, engineers looked at how the plane's wiring could have sparked the fatal fire. It took a total of four years to figure out what probably had happened inside the cockpit that fateful day in September 1998.

Arcing — a spark that jumps from one wire to another — caused the insulation around the wires to ignite. (The insulation, it was discovered, was sub-standard and flammable.) Fire raced, undetected and unstoppable, along the right side of the cockpit's ceiling. Thirteen minutes after the pilots smelled smoke, the plane's electrical systems failed. There was nowhere to go but down.

But that's not all. The arcing responsible for the tragedy was most likely from the in-flight entertainment network, a gaming unit improperly installed on the airplane. The system has since been removed from all airplanes.

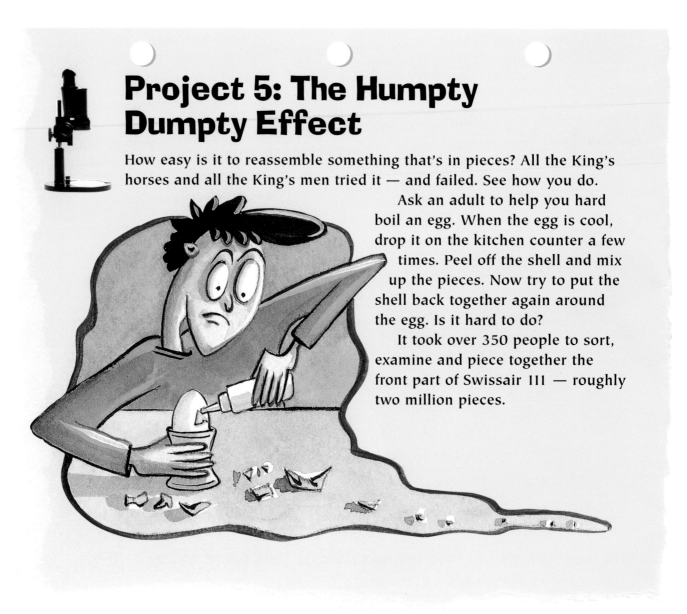

Project 5: The Humpty Dumpty Effect

How easy is it to reassemble something that's in pieces? All the King's horses and all the King's men tried it — and failed. See how you do.

Ask an adult to help you hard boil an egg. When the egg is cool, drop it on the kitchen counter a few times. Peel off the shell and mix up the pieces. Now try to put the shell back together again around the egg. Is it hard to do?

It took over 350 people to sort, examine and piece together the front part of Swissair 111 — roughly two million pieces.

Columbia Crashes

When the space shuttle *Columbia* broke up February 1, 2003, while re-entering Earth's atmosphere, over 120 investigators, four hundred NASA and contractor employees and twenty-five thousand searchers began finding the debris and re-assembling the shuttle.

Investigators watched lift-off videos over and over. It didn't take long to figure out the problem. The video showed foam insulation breaking off and hitting the shuttle. It was the first important clue, and it led engineers to the cause of the tragedy. The wreckage contained other clues — melted aluminum parts — that confirmed what engineers suspected: the foam dislodged a seal on the shuttle's left wing during lift-off. It fell off, creating a gap. When the shuttle re-entered Earth's atmosphere, the gap let in enough scorching gas to rip the ship apart. Seven crew members were lost.

Columbia was the first space shuttle to orbit Earth.

Inside a hangar at Kennedy Space Center, investigators pieced together parts of *Columbia*. The yellow grid lines helped reconstruct the space shuttle.

INDEX